CONTENTS

KU-549-601

College Voices

By **Janet Murray**

With an introduction by David Hunter, Chief Executive
Lifelong Learning UK

the**guardian**

Published by Lifelong Learning UK

Writer
Janet Murray

Designer
Dane Wilson

Editor
Diane Hofkins

Executive editor
Ezri Carlebach
Lifelong Learning UK

Project Manager
Sunita Gordon
The Guardian

Photographers
Apex
Frank Baron
Lorne Campbell
Felix Clay
Getty
John Lawrence
Sam Morgan
Linda Nylind
David Sillitoe
Gabriel Szabo
SWNS
Christopher Thomond
Graham Turner

Printed and bound in
Great Britain by
Dayfold Ltd.

First published 2009 by
Lifelong Learning UK
5th Floor, St Andrew's House
18-20 St Andrew Street
London
EC4A 3AY

ISBN 978-0-9562061-0-7

This book is published in
association with The Guardian

Interviews by Janet Murray
first published in The Guardian
2008 and 2009

ISBN 978-0-9562061-0-7
TITLE College Voices

Vision for a world class workforce

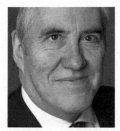

I am delighted to support the publication of this collection of College Voices, and I hope that you find something that touches you, and perhaps causes you to see colleges in a different light.

These superb stories stand in their own right as moving testimony on behalf of lifelong learning in general, and further education in particular, and its ability to bring about positive change in people's lives. They also speak directly to the quality and commitment of the workforce in the lifelong learning sector. That's why Lifelong Learning UK's work in support of that workforce, and its professionalisation and continuous development, is so valuable. It is our vision for the UK to demonstrate that it has a world class lifelong learning sector.

By 'world class' we mean a profession that can attract and retain high-calibre individuals, and that offers flexible entry routes and transferable skills. It means employers who understand and interpret the shape and nature of their workforce, and can work with us to predict skills gaps before they arise.

And it also means a sector which reflects and celebrates the diversity of the wider UK workforce in the 21st century. Lifelong Learning UK is committed to supporting the sector in achieving this vision and to ensuring that the UK's lifelong learning workforce is the best in the world.

David Hunter Chief Executive, Lifelong Learning UK

From mean streets to broadsheets

Lee McConville is on the NCTJ course in print journalism at Harlow College

I grew up in Lozells, Birmingham, which is notorious for drugs, prostitution and gang culture. There were occasions when I had to carry a knife just to protect myself. I'm lucky not to have been shot or stabbed. But I did come close. I'd get caught up in fights with the friends I hung around with and things could get ugly. One time, I had my arm slashed in a fight. Another time, I almost got shot – a car pulled up alongside me and someone pointed a gun in my face. It was a case of mistaken identity.

I left school at 16 and got a job in a warehouse. I was earning good money and life was OK. Things went wrong after my arm was slashed. I needed months of physiotherapy, so I had to sign on. I was really low, and it was then that the drinking started. I was living in a hostel – my parents had got fed up with the police coming round.

Everything seemed to go wrong at once: my girlfriend had a miscarriage, a friend was shot dead on his birthday, then another friend, two weeks later. All my anger built up and I attacked someone at the hostel. I was warned that if I didn't sort myself out, I'd have to leave.

They put me in touch with the charity Fairbridge, which supports young people not in education or training. I got involved with a media project that involved shooting a film about life in Lozells, which was brilliant. At the London Imax screening I gave a speech to 300 people working in the media and appealed for work experience.

A few months later, the Media Trust asked if I'd like to be part of a youth mentoring programme, which would involve a trip to Germany for the G8 summit. I was paired with Philip Webster, the political editor at The Times. It was an amazing experience. There I was, a young guy from Lozells, sitting 15 feet away from George Bush and Tony Blair.

While I was out there, I kept a video diary for the community TV channel and wrote a feature for Times Online. I was interviewed on Richard and Judy, ITV's On The Couch and various radio stations. The experience gave me a taste for journalism. I'd had the idea that politics had nothing to do with people in deprived communities like Lozells. It has everything to do with them.

I wanted a career in journalism, and I found out that the National Council for the Training of Journalists has a diversity fund. I passed the pre-entry examination for the year-long NCTJ course at Harlow College, Essex, and was awarded a bursary. I started in September 2008. I'm still in touch with my mentor, Philip, who has been there for me every step of the way. I'm 23 now and finally getting my life on track.

Where I was brought up, everything was about money. It would have been so easy to turn to the streets to make money, but now I can see a different kind of future.

Recognising the youth workers

Without his time at Fairbridge, Lee might never have found his passion for journalism. Youth workers and youth support workers in organisations like this help young people to raise their aspirations and have their achievements recognised. Those in the Youth Work workforce can also have their achievements and professionalism recognised, through a qualification based on national occupational standards produced by Lifelong Learning UK.

Steve Belcher (charity worker)

Lee came to us at a really low point in his life. His turning point was a film-making course run by Fairbridge which really captured his interest. As a result, his confidence levels rose and his natural leadership skills came through.

Each year Fairbridge helps over 3,700 marginalised young people aged 13-25 turn their lives around, through one-to-one support and group courses, ranging from interpersonal skills to health and independent living. We also run projects which give young people the chance to develop skills in sports, creative and performing arts and other recreational areas.

We have 16 centres in some of the most disadvantaged areas of England, Scotland and Wales.

Our goal is to enable young people to develop the confidence, motivation and life skills they need to engage with education or employment. Many of the young people we work with have never received the encouragement and opportunities that most of us take for granted. We provide a first step, someone to believe in them and a fair chance to prove themselves.

Lee stills pops into the Fairbridge centre when he's back in Birmingham. He is an inspiration and demonstrates that young people can change their lifestyles, make better choices and challenge themselves to make different decisions.

Steve Belcher is outreach & development worker, Fairbridge West Midlands www.fairbridge.org.uk

A lifeline through tough times

Pam Frew is curriculum administrator for adult and community courses at Harrow College

I've been working at the college since 1987, when adult education was usually referred to as 'night school'. Although a lot has changed in adult education since then, I'm doing virtually the same job, putting on recreational courses for people in the local community both at Harrow College and other local venues.

We offer everything from languages to dressmaking to salsa dancing. Increasingly, our courses are influenced by trends, particularly TV programmes, so there is a big demand for singing and ballroom dancing classes at the moment. Because of the BBC's Who Do You Think You Are, people are increasingly interested in family history, so genealogy is popular too.

We get a lot of our ideas from the public. If someone phones up and asks about a course or subject we don't offer, we'll see if it's viable. I think we offer an invaluable service to the community. As well as learning, there is also the opportunity to socialise with like-minded people which is very important.

But funding cuts mean the sector is shrinking. I was particularly sad when concessionary rates for over sixties were stopped a few years ago, as adult and community education is particularly valuable for this age group.

My work has kept me going through some difficult times. Back in 1996, I found a lump in my breast. My body had never let me down. I couldn't believe there could be anything wrong. I was so convinced of this, after my GP referred me to a hospital consultant, I went to the appointment on my own.

It all happened very quickly. I had a needle biopsy, ultrasound and diagnosis of cancer, all on the same day. I was booked in for a full biopsy the following week. Later that month I had a mastectomy and started chemotherapy shortly afterwards.

When trauma hits you like that, it's the first thing you think of when you wake up in the morning, the last thing you think of at night. On the day of my mastectomy, my eldest daughter had a GCSE exam. The youngest was going on a school trip. But I was determined for things to carry on as normal. I was most worried for my parents, who were in their seventies. We're a close family and they took it very hard.

I had six months of chemotherapy. I continued going to work as much as I could. Keeping busy with work and my hobby, boating, has kept me going. I've even taken some classes here including IT, salsa and pilates. When I pop into classes and see people enjoying themselves and reaping the benefits of education, it's very satisfying.

Begin with a beguine
People who have struggled to gain qualifications can – and do – get back into learning through recreational courses. It's as much a question of self-belief as academic ability.

David Hunter, CEO of Lifelong Learning UK, says: 'I was an adult education co-ordinator in Belfast and saw how people came into education and moved through by taking bite-sized chunks.

They might originally start with ballroom dancing then move on to art or a technical skill as their confidence developed.'

Shirley Boyle (student)

I started doing adult community learning courses in my late fifties, after a 30-year break from education. Four years earlier, my 20-year-old son had died, in very traumatic circumstances. I'd become isolated at home. As well as building my confidence back up, I needed to get out and meet people.

Over the next few years, I did a number of day-time courses at Harrow including Confidence, Assertiveness and Self-esteem and Speaking With Confidence. One course I did was aimed at unemployed people, helping them get back into work. Another was for local business women. So they couldn't have been more different. Mixing with different kinds of people was just what I needed at that time.

After the classes, we'd all go for lunch together. It helped me get back into the 'real world'.

As my confidence grew, I began thinking about going back to education full-time. It was something I'd wanted to do at 40, but was worried about how I would manage financially.

After my son's death, I realised life was too short. Two years ago, I sold my house to fund myself through a foundation degree in counselling. It was hard emptying my home and moving on after so many years, but I'm so glad I did it.

If I hadn't taken that first step and tried the confidence courses at college, I wouldn't be where I am I now. Now I feel life is full of possibilities.

Shirley Boyle is studying for a foundation degree (Fda) in Counselling at Harrow College

'My mum would have been incredibly proud'

Suzanna Branco is studying for a foundation degree in performing arts (drama and theatre) at Barnet College

My mum always said I was a drama queen. She sent me to acting classes when I was 10. I did drama classes and productions at the Young Vic and Bridewell theatres in London. My family all have sensible jobs, but from an early age, I knew I wanted to perform.

Nevertheless, I thought it would be good to have a back-up plan, so I started a degree in film studies and philosophy. I dropped out after a year and started a foundation degree in performing arts at college.

I was 19 when my mum developed breast cancer. It all happened very quickly; despite chemotherapy, within six months of the diagnosis the disease had spread to her bones, liver and lungs. My brother was thirteen and my sister just two years old.

I felt so angry. Mum had noticed the lump a few months after my little sister was born, but doctors had her fobbed her off, saying it was just a blocked milk duct, where she was breastfeeding. I can't help wondering what would have happened if it had been diagnosed earlier.

When she died, I was three weeks away from the opening night of a play I was doing with the Young Person's Theatre Company in Camden, north London. People were surprised when I said I was going ahead with the play. When she was ill, my mum encouraged us all to carry on normally. I was playing one of the main parts and I didn't want to let people down. I knew if I could channel my energy into my performance, it would help me deal with the pain. The opening night was just a week after my mum's funeral.

Two years on, it hasn't got any easier. You just learn to deal with the pain. The first set of birthdays and Christmas was really hard. Until she met my step-dad, my mum had brought me up alone, so we were very close. You grow up thinking that your mum is like the Iron Man, always there to help you. She was in so much pain. By the end, I was praying for her to die, just so she didn't have to suffer.

It's hard knowing that she won't be there for my wedding, her first grandchild. I know she would have been proud to see my brother start college recently and my sister start nursery.

Since she died, I've taken on a more motherly role in the family. My little sister needs lots of cuddles. And although my step-dad is around, there are some things my teenage brother prefers to talk to me about, like girls.

My friends and teachers at college have been brilliant, really supportive. Sometimes it's hard when I hear my friends moaning about their mums, but I've told them they should behave normally around me. I don't want to be treated any differently. I keep busy with college, my theatre group and my part-time job in a shoe shop. Mum would have wanted it that way.

This summer I am off to New York, to spend a month studying at the New York Conservatory in Performing Arts (of Fame) on a free scholarship. I auditioned last year and there were sixty hopefuls just in two hours I was there. I couldn't believe I'd been picked out from so many performers. My mum would have been incredibly proud.

Something that matters
There is no doubt that further education has an impact on the economy and on students' economic prospects. The key point for Suzanna, however, is that FE helps give a sense of community and belonging.

In a Lifelong Learning UK-sponsored Guardian supplement in February 2009, Alan Tuckett, director of the National Institute of Adult Continuing Education (NIACE), expanded on this idea. Through education, he wrote, adults who are out of work 'regained confidence through opportunities to do something meaningful and stimulating – whether in the pursuit of a personal interest, or by working with others to make a difference to their communities. This is true of everyone outside the paid workforce – and is the reason why, for a century, colleges and community educators offered a combination of learning for work and learning for a life worth living. Time now, I think, for a renaissance of that ethos.'

Revelling in the wonder of every day things

Sam Dunn is studying AS-levels in geology, physics and maths and A2 chemistry at St Austell College, Cornwall.

What I love about science is the endless possibilities. It is such a vast, creative subject. It makes you see the world differently. I'm so enthusiastic about science, I started AS-level chemistry at 15.

I was one of four students chosen to take part in an experiment with Cornwall College to see if GCSE students who performed well in science could handle the workload of a more challenging exam. I got an A* in my chemistry GCSE and 79% in my AS level – just one mark off an A – which means I should be on course for an A at A2 level.

I was surprised to be selected for the project. Although I've always enjoyed science, I wouldn't have said I was the smartest at science in my year group. But when the others dropped out because of the workload, I managed to keep going.

Meanwhile, I was working really hard on my English. My reading is good, but I've always struggled with spelling and getting my ideas organised, so essay-based subjects such as English, history and geography are quite tough

for me. During my GCSE year, I was diagnosed with dyslexia, which meant I got extra time in the exams. I came out with B grades in English and English literature, so I was really pleased with that.

I went to the college to study AS chemistry several times a week. At first, it was daunting sitting in lessons with older students, but I felt really welcome and the college couldn't do enough to make me feel comfortable. I even joined them on a week-long trip to Switzerland over the summer to study pharmaceuticals at Basel University. Tackling university-level work was another big challenge, but I enjoyed every minute.

Science is all around us. Since I started studying chemistry, whenever I go into a supermarket I read the back of food packets; all those weird names, which used to make no sense. Now I can start to understand where they come from and how they are made.

Then there is plastic: so many of the things we use on a daily basis contain or are made of plastic. That all starts with chemistry. I've just started AS levels in geology, physics and maths and A2 chemistry at college. Chemistry is definitely my passion. That's what I'd like to study at university and I hope to pursue a career in that field.

I'm glad to hear the project is going to be happening again next year, this time with up to eight students.

Partnerships for growth

The growing numbers of students taking science at AS and A-level have fed through to further and higher education. UCAS figures show significant increases in applications to study STEM subjects – science, technology, engineering and mathematics. This has not been achieved by schools and colleges working in isolation, but is about working in partnership. It relates to the government's ambition to develop the country's skills base, so that the UK produces succeeding generations of talented young scientists and technologists.

Harley Rosser-James (tutor) Studying like this means you can work at your own pace. If you're finding it particularly easy, you can move onto the next level, set yourself a new challenge, which isn't always possible in a school setting. I'm really grateful to the college for letting me take my study of chemistry to the next level.

It's really important for us to work with local schools as many of their students come to us for sixth form studies. A number of our staff teach science in local 'partner' schools and their students come here for science events. If we can get the most talented, able students enthusiastic about science early on, we hope that interest will be maintained.

Getting schools and colleges working closely together is a key part of the 14-19 agenda. Students like coming here because, as a large college, we generally have better equipment and facilities than their schools.

Some of our academic staff have specialisms, so there is a chance to find out a bit more about certain topics.

As well as stretching the most able students, having an AS level under their belt by the time they finish GCSEs opens up opportunities.

They can pick up an additional subject in sixth form, which might help with future career choices.

Sam is passionate about his studies and committed to a career in science. At the beginning, he was quite apprehensive about making the leap to AS level, but he did really well in the first set of exams. He really blossomed as a result.

Harley Rosser-James, is head of science, Cornwall College

Determined to be a doctor

Emma Graney studied A-levels in maths, biology, chemistry and psychology at King George V College, Southport. She has won an Association of Colleges' student of the year award

I became a carer when I was eight. My mum had a bowel disorder and various health conditions. Sometimes she'd be bedridden for weeks at a time. At first my nan used to help out a lot. Then she developed lung cancer, so I was helping out with both of them.

My nan died when I was 11, so I was on my own after that. My dad wasn't around and there wasn't any other family I was aware of.

From an early age, I walked myself to and from school, did some of the shopping and cooked all my dinners, usually scrambled eggs or micro-waved noodles. The teachers noticed and used to help me out, giving me lifts home from after-school clubs when it was dark.

I didn't really talk about the situation at home. I felt awkward and embarrassed. Instead, I buried myself in my school work. I loved maths from an early age. When I was at home, ill, I used to write to the teachers to ask for work.

When I was 15, my relationship with my mum broke down and she asked me to leave. I went to a friend's house and her parents put me up for three months, which was really kind of them.

The teachers at school put me in touch with the Merseyside Accommodation Project. As well as giving me advice on independent living, when I turned 16 they helped me to find accommodation in supported lodgings, where you live semi-independently within a family home. Over the next few years, I lodged in four different places and spent some time in a bed and breakfast. Again, my teachers were really supportive. Two even invited me round for dinner.

At 18, I moved into my own flat. It was a bit strange going back to the flat on my own every night. I spent a lot of time studying in the local library. I was there until closing time and the staff knew me by name. It sounds clichéd but my situation gave me the determination to succeed. I passed my A-levels with straight As and I'm now studying medicine at Queen's University, Belfast.

Living in halls is much better than the flat. There's always someone to talk to. Money is tight though, and I've got two part-time jobs. If I save up a lot this year, I'll be able to cut down on part-time work in subsequent years, when the workload will go up. Things are getting back on track with my mum now, which is great. Special occasions are still tricky though. There's never any shortage of offers from friends, but I don't like to intrude on people's family time. People have shown me such kindness over the years: teachers, friends and their parents. I'm so grateful for that.

Gateways to learning
Libraries are a vital community resource. They offer learning opportunities ranging from adult literacy classes to the World Wide Web. 'Libraries have a pivotal role that isn't always fully recognised,' says Michelle Creed, Lifelong Learning UK director for Wales. 'They play an essential role in our basic skills agenda and lifelong learning.'

LLUK represents librarians, archivists and information service providers working in public libraries where the primary purpose is the support or delivery of lifelong learning, and in universities and colleges, across the UK and has developed National Occupational Standards in these fields to ensure staff can help students like Emma reach their goals.

Lisa Randall (teacher)

When Emma first arrived at college, she stood out immediately. She was so enthusiastic about learning. She was always well-prepared for lessons and often stayed behind afterwards to ask questions.

As I got to know her, she began to talk more about her personal circumstances. In the second year she was with us, I became her personal tutor. At our college, all students meet with their tutor once a week to discuss their progress and any concerns they might have. We also operate an open door policy, so I met with Emma several times a week. She really valued having someone she could talk to.

The college has a Solo Support worker, who can provide help with finding accommodation, accessing benefits and practical matters. We helped her move and staff donated furniture for her new flat. During her time at the college, Emma was nominated for a number of awards, so I took her down to London for the award ceremonies.

Emma was so keen to get a university place to study medicine, she spent all her free time volunteering. She worked for the children's charity Barnardo's as a befriender, meeting with a lady with special needs every fortnight. She pushed a tea trolley round the local hospital and helped on holiday play schemes.

Many young people in Emma's situation would have lost focus. Her determination to succeed is a real inspiration.

Lisa Randall is a psychology teacher and personal tutor at King George V College, Southport

Turning know how into teaching

Steven Kendall is the pre-apprenticeship manager for built environment at Camborne College, Cornwall

I wanted to be a building surveyor from a very early age. My dad was a carpenter, a general foreman on new house builds. As a child, I used to go to work with him at weekends, passing him tools and generally helping out.

When I was 15, my dad died. I just went into freefall. My dad had been suffering from motor neurone disease, which leads to weakness and wasting of muscles, loss of mobility in the limbs, and difficulties with speech, swallowing and breathing. Over a number of years, I'd seen my dad go into a vegetative state.

When he died, I lost focus at school and didn't do very well in my exams, so that was the end of my plans to become a surveyor. Fortunately, a man in my village offered me an apprenticeship as a carpenter, which I loved.

In 2001, I started thinking about teaching. Customers were always asking me to show them how to do the things they were paying me for. My wife said I was putting myself out of business. She encouraged me to ask the college if they had any teaching jobs. I've been here ever since.

I'm course manager for pre-apprenticeship courses for 14- to 18-year-olds. We have 45 places for 14- to 16-year-olds from local schools. They come to us one day a week and work towards vocational qualifications, including the City & Guilds' introductory certificate in construction and the BTec first diploma in construction.

They learn a bit of everything: health and safety, manual handling, carpentry, masonry, painting and decorating. Some students come to us because the school environment doesn't suit them. They find sitting in a classroom day in, day out really difficult. I can relate to that, as I found school difficult, particularly as I have dyslexia. We have some students who are a nightmare at school, but get on great in the college environment, where they are on first-name terms with the teachers. For some, being in a more adult environment is really motivating and has a knock-on effect on their behaviour in school.

At the moment, we don't have any young women on our pre-construction courses. I'm trying to recruit some more girls by going out to visit local schools. The old stereotypes about girls going into beauty and hairdressing still stand.

Last month, I organised an open day for 50 girls from local schools who were about to choose their GCSE options. As well as driving a mini-digger, they did some painting and decorating, and soldered pipes in a plumbing workshop. They also had the opportunity to speak to females in the industry, including surveyors, engineers, apprentice plumbers, electricians and construction workers. They all got stuck in and really enjoyed it. At the end of the day, the majority said they would definitely consider a career in construction.

I've got four daughters, aged seven to 20. I'm keen for them to stay open-minded about possible careers. Most girls have never considered a career in construction. They have little knowledge of the variety of jobs available. If we can get them started early, there's a better chance they'll give it a go.

Pass On Your Skills

Pass on Your Skills is part of the Catalyst programme of recruitment and staff development initiatives for the further education sector in England, run by Lifelong Learning UK.

In 2008 the Pass On Your Skills project ran a pilot scheme targeting shortages in the health and social care and engineering sectors.

This resulted in 2,500 eligible candidates being registered.

Following from this success, in 2009 LLUK is focusing on construction and the built environment in the hope of bringing more people with relevant industry experience like Steven into colleges. It is also targeting STEM subjects (science, technology engineering and maths), skills for life (literacy and numeracy), retail and commercial services and health and social care.

And with equality and diversity at the heart of everything LLUK does, it will encourage women as well as men to teach, and learn, construction skills.

Catalyst comprises Pass On Your Skills and three other key areas.

Make a Difference encourages motivated graduate calibre individuals to build a management career in further education.

Business Interchange gives FE staff the chance to update their skills in industry by working more closely with local businesses through work based placements.

Animated by the movie business

Alan McKenna completed a first national diploma in media and A-level film studies at Bury College

I always knew I was different. I started to come to terms with it when I was in secondary school. The other students picked on me. After a few months, I was transferred to a special needs school.

I got on much better there. It was much smaller. I have Asperger's syndrome, a form of autism, which makes communication and social relationships difficult. It can also be hard to adapt to new situations. I find it hard to read people's emotions. For example, sometimes it is hard for me to tell if people are joking or serious. Noisy, busy places can make me anxious. Socialising isn't easy, especially in busy places like the cinema, but I am getting better at those.

I had a girlfriend for a while, but it was difficult because sometimes I just want to be by myself. I wanted my own space. Another problem is that I sometimes lose track of time, which can be hard for others to understand.

I can get stressed out working with other people. I get overwhelmed and I don't know what to say. I can get shaky, blurt out things and even lash out.

School was great, but there weren't too many GCSEs on offer. I decided to go on to college to further my education. When I started college, I was doing vocational studies, which was all about getting ready for working life.

Meeting new people is hard for me, but I am much better at it now. At college, I had a support worker, who helped me to cope. She explained what people were feeling and their attitudes.

Even at college, people weren't always nice. They'd make out they couldn't understand my speech or laugh at me. I'd get steamed up. It really helped to have a support worker to talk to.

I've always been good at maths, but I find English difficult, especially spelling. I also write very slowly. It took a few years to get my English GCSE, but I finally got there. I was so pleased when I got a C.

Then I went on to a BTec in media, which was when I really got into animation. I completed a first national diploma in media with distinction and got a B in A-level film studies. It has taken me five years, but I've done it.

I'm now starting a degree in animation at Salford University. I am so excited to be taking this step, to be taking on a new challenge. I want to work in TV or in the film industry, maybe as a writer or director.

I am a bit nervous about meeting new people, but I think college has helped a lot. When I was younger, I'd get anxious if I didn't know what was happening next, which is common with Asperger's. Now I'm far more used to change. I even like surprises.

An e-capable workforce
Lifelong Learning UK helps ensure the lifelong learning workforce is competent with new technology. Staff need to have the tools and skills to make the most of IT so it is used to enhance learning and services. This means people like Alan can receive the specific education they need in order to achieve their dreams.

Both general and professional IT skill shortages have been identified in lifelong learning establishments. Unless the workforce is e-capable and e-confident, they will be unable to meet the needs of students as they become more technically adept.

Alistair McNaught

Traditionally education has been firmly text driven, with lots of reading and writing based assessment. This means disabled people or those with learning disabilities can get a raw deal. TechDis is a free advisory service which aims to support teachers and learners, making the education sector as accessible and inclusive as possible.

One of the things we do is provide free information and resources to help teachers adapt their learning resources to cater for learners with different needs.

For example, we provide step-by-step instructions showing teachers how to make documents and presentations which can be easily converted to mind maps; these can be helpful to deaf or dyslexic learners. It shouldn't take the teacher any more time, it's just making the best use of resources they already have. We also collect and collate free tools teachers can use to make their resources more inclusive.

Our website contains information about innovative techniques and examples of good practice.

In one recently trialled project, students were given a memory stick they could plug into any computer which contained text-to-speech software. Like podcasting, this kind of approach can work really well for dyslexic students or those who find it difficult to concentrate for long periods of time. Instead of ploughing through the course notes, they can listen to them at home or even on the go.

Alistair McNaught is Senior Advisor at JISC TechDis
www.techdis.ac.uk

The confidence to be a teacher

Sam Cox is studying hairdressing NVQ level 3 at Somerset College

I was bullied at primary school, with two of my friends. It was the usual story: name-calling, isolating us from others. There were five of them, all girls, and they controlled the whole class. When it became apparent the head wasn't going to do anything, our parents took us out of school.

When my parents decided I was going to be home educated, my mum sat down with me and worked out a timetable. We worked around the 'school day', with a break for lunch. It really worked for me. I'm dyslexic, so having one-to-one help was brilliant. If I didn't understand something, I could ask my mum to go over it. At school, I didn't always want to admit I didn't understand something, especially when I was being bullied.

Being home educated meant we could move on more quickly with the subjects I was good at. I really like history, so we were able to choose subjects I found the most interesting. Of course, there were days when I woke up and couldn't be bothered to learn, but my mum was very firm with me. I'm grateful for that.

The subject I didn't really enjoy was science. We did a lot of theory. My mum did buy some experiments from a home-education organisation, so we tried a few out in the kitchen, but it wasn't the same as it would have been at school.

Hearing what secondary school was like from my friends made me glad I was at home. They'd talk about classes of 32, where one child who was misbehaving got all the attention.

I didn't miss out on socialising. Once a month we'd get together with other families who were home educated and go on visits to museums and even a local ice rink. Evenings and weekends I was always busy, at scouts, swimming or at my reading group.

Starting college was quite daunting at first. After being educated at home for five years, I was worried about the size of the place and the number of people. Despite being in a class of 20, I settled in quickly and my tutors were brilliant. There were three of us with dyslexia, so we had a learning support assistant to take notes for us. In the past, I'd tried to hide my dyslexia. In the college environment, everyone is more accepting.

Having completed hairdressing NVQ level 1 and 2, I'm doing level 3. Then I hope to train as an NVQ assessor and eventually train to teach at FE colleges.

Being bullied was horrible, but it's been a blessing in disguise. I'm stronger now. If my parents hadn't taken me out of school, I think the experience would have destroyed my confidence. I'm very satisfied with what I've achieved.

Thinking about teaching?
If, like Sam, you want to teach in the further education sector, you can find out what it's like before committing yourself by taking a Preparing to Teach in the Lifelong Learning Sector (PTLLS) award. It's a short course, offered in various flexible formats, which lets you learn about the basics of teaching and develop teaching skills in a supportive environment.

The course helps students to build up their knowledge of the principles of learning, teaching, assessment and evaluation; develop their own communication and interpersonal skills and consider their professional role and the value systems which underpin it.

Dawn Williams (tutor)

Hairdressing is a job which requires people skills. When Sam first came to us, having been home tutored for five years, she was very quiet and nervous, so I knew we needed to work on building her confidence.

I taught Sam hairdressing theory. People tend to see hairdressing as a practical subject. What a lot of people don't realise is you can't colour or use treatments on people's hair without understanding the science behind it. Dyslexic students can find the theory side of the course more challenging.

It's important not to make students feel singled out, so you do have to handle things sensitively. I organised a note taker to jot down notes during lessons and type them up for students who needed them. Where possible, the dyslexic students were given an option to do theory assessments verbally.

I've studied for the Certificate in Education (Cert Ed) and I have my A1 assessor award. I still draw on my initial training for lesson planning. You have to consider the needs of every student you are teaching and plan for that. At the beginning of

a course, we do a lot of small group work so quieter students can build confidence voicing their ideas to their peers. By the end, they are giving presentations to the whole class.

We got Sam a placement at a local hair salon one day a week. Dealing with clients and mixing with colleagues in the workplace was brilliant for her. Two years on, she is much more confident and self-assured.

Dawn Williams is personal tutor, hair and beauty, at Somerset College

'I thought I would never see daylight again'

Aime Youba has completed the BTec national diploma in public services at City College Brighton and Hove

I was arrested and imprisoned in Cameroon when I was 16, along with my mother, father and sister. We were at home one night, when the police came. It is difficult for me to talk about what happened that night, but it was very violent. We were driven to a prison, miles from our home and separated. I was kept in the dark, alone for a month. I thought I would never see daylight again.

Because I was young, I didn't fully understand the situation. My father was a university lecturer. He was also in politics, a member of the opposition party in Cameroon, the Social Democratic Front.

A contact of my father, who was working at the prison at the time, helped me escape. He told me a day and time he would leave the doors and gates unlocked. I left when it was dark and headed for my village. My family had only moved there a few months earlier, so it was difficult to find my way back. I walked all night and arrived in the morning.

I headed straight for my auntie's house but she didn't really want me to stay because the police had already been there, looking for me. She arranged for me to stay at a friend's house. It was a different kind of prison; I had food and water and nice people around me, but I couldn't leave the house.

Two weeks later, my auntie came to see me. The police were still looking for me and they had arrested my uncle. She said I must leave the country. She came back three days later with a white lady, who arranged papers and a passport for me. Two days later I landed in Gatwick airport. I was met by a friend of my auntie's, who brought me to Brighton. I stayed with her for a little while, before the council arranged for me to stay in a hostel.

At first I was relieved that I was safe, that I was not in danger any more. Then the anxiety started. I was in a new country, spoke very little English and everything was new to me. I had no idea what had happened to my family. I fell into a deep depression.

The hostel workers were wonderful. They were so caring and supportive, always there to listen. I was so traumatised by what I had seen and experienced, they arranged counselling sessions for me, which I had for a year. Nevertheless, I was keen to continue my education.

With the help of my social worker, I enrolled at college in Brighton. I did a one year English course full-time. Afterwards I moved onto the public service course. I have always been interested in working in public services, particularly in the police. I want to contribute something positive to the community. I passed the course and am now working as a security officer in shops around East Sussex. It's not the most interesting work, but I'm building up experience so I can apply for the police force.

I still don't know what has happened to my family back in Cameroon. I'd love to go back and look for them, but until I get a British passport, hopefully in the next year or so, I don't think it would be safe.

I'm 21 now and I live in Brighton, with my girlfriend and seven-month-old son. They are the only good thing to come out of this. Being a father gives me hope and something to look forward to.

Equality and diversity

Education should lay the foundations for a better world. The FE sector is committed to supporting social cohesion and global citizenship; understanding and meeting the needs of learners from all backgrounds; and ensuring that staff reflect the diversity of learners and communities.

Colleges seek to reduce social exclusion and widen access to learning. They attract learners and workers from wide and varied backgrounds. By promoting equality and diversity, Lifelong Learning UK is supporting the sector in removing barriers to employment and recognising the value of a diverse workforce.

The Workforce Race Advisory Group, led by LLUK, advises the government on issues of race equality for FE staff. In its publication Race Equality in Further Education Colleges, WRAG's predecessor, the Commission for Black Staff in Further Education, states:

'For colleges, with their remit to address skills shortages and under-representation, asylum seekers represent a largely untapped, frequently multi-lingual human resource. Many arrive in the UK fully trained, yet their skills, experience and professional qualifications continue to go largely unrecognised due to real or perceived language barriers. Far from lowering standards, they are among the most highly motivated employees and the most exceptional students.

'Colleges also face the challenge of countering negative, xenophobic attitudes towards vulnerable individuals and isolated communities. This requires a raised awareness of the reasons why asylum seekers left home and the vital role FE can play in honouring Britain's commitment to the European Convention on Human Rights.'

www.lluk.org/3151.htm

Finally travelling on the right road

Jess Redel is a lecturer in travel and tourism at South Nottingham College

School didn't work for me. At times, I felt invisible. No matter how hard I tried, the teachers didn't notice me. I did get nine GCSEs, but they were mostly Cs. Being 'in the middle' you tend to get overlooked. At least, that was how it felt to me.

I started suffering from depression when I was about 13, following a viral illness. I didn't want to get out of bed, I just couldn't get excited about anything. Everything just seemed so pointless. I had counselling and, with the support of my family, struggled on until I left school.

After GCSEs, my teachers said there was no point in staying at school to do A-levels as I wouldn't do very well. That really knocked my confidence. But it actually turned out to be the making of me.

I'd always been interested in travel, so I enrolled on an Advanced Certificate of Vocational Education (AVCE) in travel and tourism at South Nottingham College. It couldn't have been more different from school. The teachers were enthusiastic about their subject and really positive and encouraging. When my first piece of work came back, my tutor kept saying how good it was. It was the first time a teacher had ever praised me. They regularly told us we could do anything we wanted if we were prepared to work hard. I found it so motivating.

After that, I went from strength to strength. The high point of the two year course was a residential trip to Gambia. We were split into groups and we all had to devise a programme of activities for one day of the trip, starting with breakfast and finishing with evening entertainment. A few of us were taken to meet some families in a local village called Sekuta. It was a big eye opener. The children had no toys so they were playing with old tyres and other junk, but they were very happy. Back in the UK, children want everything, but they are still not happy.

It was a real turning point for me. Visiting the Gambia made me appreciate everything I had, all the opportunities open to me. I began to overcome my depression. I went on to get a double A grade for my AVCE and started a HND at Loughborough College, which I later topped up to a degree.

While I was studying towards my degree, I started working at the college. I started off as a volunteer, helping out in classes a few hours a week. Then I was asked to take on three hours' teaching a week on the AVCE travel and tourism course. I was absolutely thrilled.

I got a first in my degree. I was so proud. Then the college asked me to take on some more teaching. I now teach 17 hours a week and have completed a college teaching qualification. I've also been back to the Gambia eight times.

Each year, our principal funds two students from the Gambia to study travel and tourism at the college. The idea is that the students can take what they've learned back to their own country. I've been helping set up a travel and tourism training school course in the Gambia, funded by South Nottingham College. The aim is to give local people there the opportunity to develop tourism in their own country.

Becoming a teacher in the lifelong learning sector

Good teachers can make all the difference. Jess's experience as a travel and tourism student enabled her to set out on a path that ultimately led to a degree and a job as a lecturer herself. Lifelong Learning UK sets the standards and provides the qualifications framework to equip trainees to become inspirational teachers.

If you want to become an FE teacher, you could work in a variety of learning environments, ranging from FE colleges and adult and community centres to prisons. The types of courses you could teach include academic subjects such as maths, history or psychology or vocational courses which train students for careers in catering, construction or childcare.

To become a teacher in the lifelong learning sector, you would need at least a level 3 qualification, such as an A-level or NVQ in your subject, and to complete a teaching endorsed qualification.

'When my children reached school age I knew it was my time'

Asha Khemka is the principal and chief executive of West Nottinghamshire College

I was engaged at 14 and married at 15. It was an arranged marriage. I only met my husband, a first-year medical student, a couple of months before the wedding. Where I come from, a traditional village in Rajasthan, in north-west India, stories like mine are very common. By the time I was 19, I had three children.

We moved to the UK in 1978. My husband had a job at the Royal Orthopaedic hospital in Birmingham. It was a big change for me. When we first arrived, it was snowing. I knew very little English and there were big adjustments to make. In India, if you can afford it, you have servants. Here, I had to do everything: cooking, cleaning, washing.

Most of all, I missed my nanny. At home, I'd been able to sit around while my nanny looked after the children. Suddenly, I had three young children to look after, all by myself. The children were very used to their nanny. The youngest gave me a hard time at first.

My children were very bright. When they reached school age, they all won scholarships to public schools. Then I knew it was my time. I finished my education at college and did a business studies degree at Cardiff University. Afterwards, I got a job as a college lecturer. Over the next 10 years, I progressed up the career ladder to college principal.

After 20 years as a housewife, I thoroughly enjoyed building up my career. What I love most about my job is making a difference, feeling that I'm taking a lead in changing the local community.

This is largely a white working-class area, one that is still recovering from the closure of the mines and the decline of the local textile industries. You can be dealing with three generations of feelings of worthlessness. What we're trying to do is widen horizons and raise aspirations. The students are my driving force.

Making the move into management

Make a Difference is one of the four programmes collectively known as Catalyst run by Lifelong Learning UK.

Make a Difference aims to support the development of a world-class management system for the further education sector by recruiting very talented people from within or outside the sector and equipping them with the knowledge, skills and understanding to become future leaders.

It will achieve this by recruiting experienced and motivated graduate-calibre individuals like Asha, matching them with management vacancies in further education and providing each with a funded leadership development programme for the first year of employment.

Alan Clarke, sector engagement manager for Lifelong Learning UK, said: 'I think the current economic climate is a factor. People are now realising that they have transferable skills. It's difficult to identify what motivates everyone, but some people want to give something back to society and others are seeking more secure employment.'

A secret artist steps into the light

John Colahan is studying for a foundation degree in arts and wellbeing at City College Norwich

I didn't enjoy school. I liked the social part, but I found learning difficult. My mum died when I was 14. That made me even more convinced that I didn't want to stay in education. I left at 16 and worked in pubs, restaurants and hotels, mostly bar work.

My mum was very creative. She was always making things and was known locally for her talent in arts and crafts. I inherited her passion for art, but as a child I was teased about it. When I brought something in to school I'd made, my classmates would say 'your mum made that'. So for many years, I was a secret artist, drawing and making things at home.

I joined the RAF in my early twenties and trained as a Flight Operations Assistant. I loved the work and being in the RAF. It also gave me the opportunity to see the world. During my 13 year career, I was posted to Germany, Sweden, Spain, America and Canada.

I particularly liked the sense of community. I stopped being a 'secret artist' and started helping out with RAF theatre groups, designing sets and promotional materials.

But you do lose touch with the real world. When you are posted to a new location, you just need to make one phone call and your accommodation is arranged for you. Your rent and council tax are taken at source, so apart from food and bills your money is pretty much your own.

When my marriage broke down, things started to go wrong. Left with three young children to raise alone, I found it difficult to cope. Because I did shift work, I found it hard to find a childminder. When I finally found one, it cost me more than I was earning. When you are in the forces, you are essentially 'on duty' 24 hours a day. I'd get called out in the night and there would be no one to look after the children.

I struggled on for 18 months, but my work was suffering. Where I'd always scored the highest grades in performance reviews, I was sliding towards the lowest. I was drinking too much, debts were piling up and I was suffering from depression. Because I wasn't thinking clearly, it never occurred to me to ask for help. If I hadn't made the decision to leave, I think I would have been discharged on health grounds.

Leaving the RAF was hard. I had to find somewhere to live, work out how to claim benefits, pay my council tax. The years that followed are a bit of a blur. The love of a good woman saved me. I met Juliet when I was helping out in a friend's pub. She saw something in me that others couldn't see at the time. With her help, I gradually got back on my feet.

I took a job at a helicopter company for a while, doing a similar job as I had in the RAF, but my heart wasn't in it. I realised what I loved about the RAF was the camaraderie, rather than the job itself. With Juliet's encouragement, I went along to an open day at City College Norwich. That's when I found out about the arts and wellbeing foundation degree. When I read the prospectus, I felt the course had been designed with me in mind, bringing together the two things I love: art and helping people. In the long-term I'd love to work in the community, putting on art courses for people with different needs.

Starting on a new career path is very empowering. Stepping into a college after so many years out of education was so scary, but it's changed my life beyond recognition.

Learning at the 'Last Chance Saloon'

For many students, further education is a second chance to make good deficient or negative experience at school. But after many years outside education, adult learners may lack the skills and confidence to return to education and training.

A research study based in Wales for the UK-wide Teaching and Learning Research Programme found that FE college is the 'last chance saloon' for many students. Students often enter college poorly prepared for study. They lack subject knowledge, basic skills and study skills, and although they recognise that qualifications are important, they often underestimate what is necessary to achieve them.

Colleges often help them pick up the pieces and overcome their negative experiences. The report says more recognition should be given to the individualised support that teachers provide.

According to another TLRP study, learners described their relationships with tutors as the key to their learning, progress and success. The researchers say it is not simply learners who are at the heart of the system, but the learner-tutor relationship. They say policy needs to recognise and support this.

Learning and Working in Further Education in Wales www.tlrp.org/proj/jephcote. html

Policy, Learning and Inclusion in the Learning and Skills Sector http://www.tlrp.org/proj/phase111/coffield.htm

Talking the talk

Carolyn Cheasman is a speech and language therapist. She teaches courses at City Lit college, London

I started to stammer around the age of eight. No one knew except my parents and one close friend. I later learned I had interiorised stammering. Like many people who have this, I had high levels of fluency. I coped by substituting the words I wanted to use with others I found easier to say. But it had a huge impact on my life, and caused me high levels of stress.

The start of a new school year is often difficult for children who stammer because they have to keep saying their name to their new teachers. I remember dropping my ruler on the floor, so I wouldn't be seen and have to say my name out loud. I've known people who stammer to change their name to something that's easier for them to say.

Many things in my life were affected. I didn't like reading aloud in class. I never took part in school plays, even though I always wanted to. When I went to friends' houses, I found it difficult to talk to their parents. Using the phone was incredibly stressful, so I didn't initiate socialising with friends. I avoided asking for things in shops. If it was a difficult word, sometimes I'd point at what I wanted or write it down.

The turning point came as I was finishing my degree, I liked the idea of teaching, but felt I wouldn't be able to do it. I confided in a tutor at university, who referred me to speech therapy at City Lit, a centre of excellence acclaimed for its work with adult stammerers. After an initial assessment, I joined an intensive course. It was a life changing experience.

There is no magical cure for stammering, but with the right support, big improvements can be made. The first step for interiorised stammering is to face it. 'Coming out' was a big thing for me, and people were very surprised. No one had noticed I had a stammer at all. I gradually reduced the words I substituted. Over time, I became more fluent and confident.

Inspired by my experience, I decided that I wanted to become a speech and language therapist. After a two-year postgraduate course, a vacancy came up at City Lit to teach courses for adults who stammer. That was in 1979 and I've been here ever since. I've recently been nominated for the Learning and Skills Improvement Service (LSIS) Lifetime Achievement Star Award.

When people come to us, they've usually reached a turning point. Some are leaving education for the world of work, others are getting married and don't want to stammer during their vows.

We don't know the exact cause of stammering. There are many theories, but the most popular at the moment is that it is multi-factorial. It may be that some people are genetically predisposed to stammering. Sometimes there is a trigger during childhood, such as a traumatic event. Some people who stammer say they talked late, others were the youngest in a large family and say it was difficult to be heard. In my case, there was no family history or trigger event that I can recall.

It's not uncommon for children who stammer to be bullied at school. That experience can colour their life as adults. That's why it's so important that we work on the psychological as well as the physical side of stammering. I still occasionally stammer, but it no longer dominates my life. It doesn't affect the choices I make. If I think I might stammer, I go ahead and say the word anyway. Facing the fear is the key to change.

STAR turns
The Learning and Skills Improvement Service holds the STAR Awards every year to recognise and reward the unsung heroes of the further education and skills sector. So far more than 11,500 people have been recognised.

In 2008 Lifelong Learning UK sponsored the Workforce Development award, presented to the senior teacher team at North East Worcestershire College for their dedication, enthusiasm and active promotion of workforce development.

Jamal Muse (student)

I've always stammered and had speech therapy as a child, but it got worse when I was doing my A levels. I wouldn't put up my hand to answer a question in class, because I was worried about stammering. I was concerned how it would affect me when I went to university. The speech therapist at my local hospital recommended the intensive stammering course at City Lit.

The first step to improvement is telling people that you stammer. It was scary at first, but very liberating. I remember going for a university interview and warning the interviewer that I had a stammer. I didn't stammer once.

One of our tasks on the course was to go out and speak to people in 'real-life' situations, which many people who stammer avoid. We went onto the streets of London, asking strangers for directions, and asking for things in shops and cafes. In one of the exercises, we had to deliberately stammer. Most people we approached weren't the slightest bit fazed. The experience helped me move towards self-acceptance.

What was so brilliant about the course was that it didn't just deal with the physical causes of stammering. We also looked at the psychology behind it. I quickly realised that I was no less of a person just because I stammered.

I'm now the second year of a degree in maths and economics at University College, London. I still stammer sometimes, but I don't have negative feelings about it any more. Now I accept and embrace my stammer. Doing the course was revolutionary for me, a truly life-changing experience.

Jamal Muse completed an intensive stammering therapy course at City Lit in 2007

77710

Building a better future

Dean Meeking is working towards an advanced apprenticeship in wood occupations at East Berkshire College

I struggled with reading and writing at school. As the years went on, I fell further and further behind. By the time I got to secondary school, I'd pretty much given up. I was frustrated by my lack of my progress, but it was easier to misbehave than admit how much it bothered me. I messed around in lessons, back chatted the teachers; anything to draw attention away from how badly I was doing.

There was a bit of teasing from my classmates. If anyone said I was stupid, I just thumped them. By the time I got to Year 9, I was being suspended from school on a regular basis. Sometimes I was excluded internally, which meant I wasn't allowed to go to lessons. As a punishment I had to help the caretaker with odd-jobs around the school mending, fixing and painting. It wasn't a punishment to me. I've always loved working with my hands. When I was excluded externally for a week or two, I'd go to work with some of my dad's friends who worked in the building trade.

I left school at 14. My head of year suggested I try an apprenticeship. I did one day a week at a college, learning basic maths and English, and four days at a local building firm. I loved the work, but I didn't pass the apprenticeship, because I still wasn't up to scratch in the 3Rs. I'd muddled through, just like I had at school, covering up the fact I was struggling.

At 17, I joined a local design and structural engineering company called Space Cubed. My boss was pleased with my work, but was keen for me to get some professional qualifications. With their support I enrolled on a part-time carpentry course along with a refresher course in basic maths and English. Meanwhile I carried on working at Space Cubed.

When I first joined East Berkshire College, I was tested for dyslexia. After years of feeling I wasn't up to much, it was such a relief to get the diagnosis. I was given one-to-one help from a learning support assistant and there was a note taker in class to make sure I didn't miss anything.

It took me a year to get through the basic skills course that is supposed to take 10 weeks, but I got there in the end.

Three years ago, when I started college, my reading and writing were so poor, I struggled to fill out the application forms. I couldn't even spell my own address. But with the help and support of my tutors and my employer, who never stopped telling me I could do it, I have improved so much.

A couple of summers ago, I bought a book in the airport, a biography of the Kray brothers, and read it on the plane. It might sound silly to others, but it was a turning point for me. It was the first book I'd ever read and enjoyed. I read a lot now, something I never did before.

Since I started my apprenticeship, my confidence has soared. I'm completely focused on getting myself a good career. If it wasn't for college, I think I would have ended up in trouble, perhaps even in prison.

Last year, I was named apprentice of the year for construction at East Berkshire College. It was a really proud moment for me. Until I started college, I felt as if I'd failed at everything I'd tried. Now I really believe I can succeed.

Tried and tested

An apprenticeship is a structured process of skill and knowledge acquisition, and is an excellent way of gaining competence in a job. Apprenticeships go back for centuries. The first formal structures were devised in 1563. Today they are available across a wide range of sectors. Lifelong Learning UK is responsible for apprenticeship frameworks in the lifelong learning sector, covering youth work across the UK and information and library services in England and Wales.

An apprenticeship is a partnership between the learner, the employer and the training provider. For a young person like Dean, it gives recognised vocational training with national certificate, boosts potential lifetime earnings, builds in support if the going gets tough and provides a route into higher education.

'If I can do it, anyone can do it'

Alan Taylor is lecturer on the BTec national diploma in uniformed services at Loughborough College

My mother died in 1953 when I was seven. My father struggled to bring up seven children on a baker's salary and we were taken into care. For the next six years we lived in a large children's home in Lincolnshire that was divided into houses, each with 15 or 16 children, run by a woman you had to called 'Mother'.

There was emotional and physical abuse on a daily basis. Children would be hauled from their beds in the middle of the night because they'd wet themselves. They had their noses rubbed in the sheets. If we were a few minutes late from school we were beaten. I often took the blame for things so my brothers and sisters wouldn't get a hiding.

I passed the 11-plus, but I didn't get a place at grammar school. I don't think they wanted anyone from 'that home'. One year, I got a bad report for maths. My house mother told me the only thing I was good for was working as a gardener. I became disillusioned with school after that. When I was 14, we were placed with a family who really cared for us, but by that time it was too late. I left school with no qualifications.

I joined the army when I was 17. I'd been working on a farm, going nowhere. I could see myself milking cows for the rest of my life so it was the best thing I could have done. When I left after 18 years, I found it difficult to settle. I tried various jobs, from sales to working as a postman. Then I took early retirement because of my arthritis and went back to college. I did an access course at college followed by a degree in ancient history and archaeology at Leicester University.

I'm now a lecturer at Loughborough College and feel I have found my niche. Because of my experiences, I can really empathise with the students. The first thing I tell them when they come through the door is 'never say can't'. If I can do it, anyone can.

Public service diploma
This is a particularly exciting time for uniformed services lecturers, as the new 14-19 Public Service diploma will become available to all students across England from 2010. Lifelong Learning UK has been working closely with other Sector Skills Councils to ensure that the skills needed by diploma teachers are developed and maintained.

LLUK is also working in partnership with the Training and Development Agency for Schools (TDA) to ensure the right continuing professional development courses and resources are available for those involved in teaching the new 14-19 Diplomas.

Employability skills

Employers remain concerned about the lack of employability skills among those applying for jobs. These include basic literacy and numeracy as well as personal skills such as problem solving and teamwork.

Employability skills are recognised by Lifelong Learning UK to be important for a wide range of lifelong learning occupations in the future. LLUK's Skills for Life project offers practical suggestions and sources of further information to support teachers in addressing the literacy, language, numeracy and ICT needs of learners. All teachers can play a significant part in providing opportunities to develop these skills, which are important for success in FE as well as in employment.

For example, LLUK helps teachers to understand that all students have different needs. Some need extra help with literacy, language, numeracy or ICT, while others have very sophisticated skills in these areas. The teachers' awareness of this will ensure that activities will stretch and challenge some learners and avoid potentially de-motivating others.

In addition, LLUK worked collaboratively with the armed services to develop generic teacher qualifications with specific elements to meet the needs of teachers, trainers and instructors. This will ensure that the qualifications taken have currency beyond the armed service context.

Within those qualifications, trainee teachers are prepared to address the literacy, language, numeracy and ICT needs of the learners they will work with, thus developing the skills which are so important for success in employment.

Tracking down the inside story

Dinneka Smillie is studying A-levels in sociology, media studies and English language at Notre Dame Catholic sixth-form college, Leeds

It took me a while to settle into secondary school. I'd just been placed in foster care, which meant a move from one side of Leeds to the other. Many of the students knew each other from primary school, but I knew no one. I've always been a hard worker, though, and I threw myself into my school work and started to make friends.

My carer was really supportive, but of course it isn't the same as living with your family. At first, it used to bother me when I heard my friends saying they were going on a family holiday or shopping for a present for Mother's Day. It was difficult because at that sort of age, many children are still quite dependent on their parents. As I grew older, I realised that all teenagers gradually grow more independent from their parents, so I didn't feel quite so different.

Around the time I started GCSEs, I was asked if I'd like to have a mentor, an undergraduate student from Leeds Metropolitan University, to help with subjects I felt I was weak in. This was part of a programme called Stepping Stones, run by Aimhigher Leeds, aimed at helping young people in care to succeed. Aimhigher is all about encouraging young people to think about going to university, especially if not many people in their family have been through higher education.

At first I was a bit annoyed at the idea of having a mentor. I was working really hard at school and getting good results. When you're in care, you don't want to be treated as if you have a special need.

In the end, I decided to seize the opportunity and I'm so glad I did. I was paired up with a second-year mathematics student. Each week we'd meet up at a homework club at a local school. I'd take along any maths work I was struggling with and she'd help. Having one-to-one tuition was invaluable because she was able to simplify the topics I was studying and explain them in a way that made sense to me. Hearing her say there were topics she'd struggled with or didn't get first time was really reassuring.

After a few weeks, I started to look forward to homework club. My mentor also took me to an open day at Leeds University. It was good to hear about university life from someone who was actually living it. I got a C in maths. I'm not sure I'd have done that without the extra support. Overall, I got two Bs and seven Cs in my GCSEs, which I was really pleased with. In recognition of my efforts, I won a governors' award at school.

When I moved to sixth-form college, I was assigned another mentor, a journalist from BBC Radio Leeds. I'm interested in a career in journalism, so he helped me to decide which courses to apply for, and talked to me about what kind of practical experience I'd need and how to sell myself on my Ucas form.

Last year I received the Aimhigher Leeds award for student of the year. I also had the opportunity to chair a national conference and present a DVD about the Stepping Stones programme. In October, I won the Sixth Form/FE Aimhigher Learner Achievement Award.

I'm now living with my aunt and cousin, and looking forward to going to university. My carer said to me that looked-after children often don't do as well in education, but I didn't see why it should hold me back. If anything, the experience has made me more determined to succeed.

Kaya Barker (project coordinator)

The Changing Futures project has been running for four years and is all about raising aspirations for looked after children. We currently work with 24 young people from local schools and colleges in Years 10, 11 and 12. The group meets weekly, after school.

As well as doing group team-building and ICT activities, we link each young person up with a mentor from Leeds Metropolitan University. Mentors not only help with school work, but they provide a positive role model. Seeing someone reasonably close to their age getting on at university can be very inspiring. It makes it seem achievable.

We also organise trips and activities. Some young people have done the Duke of Edinburgh award. We also link in with Aimhigher for a summer school. When the young people come to us, they can be very shy. It's great to see them transform, developing confidence and self-belief.

Kaya Barker is co-ordinator of the Changing Futures project, Leeds City Learning Centres

---

Aiming for social justice

It's no wonder Secretary of State John Denham was moved when he presented Dinneka with her award.

He told the gathering: 'I believe that education is the most powerful tool we have to create a fairer Britain. Aimhigher has helped universities seek out many of the most talented young people in our society, irrespective of their background. It's right for us to work to give all young people, regardless of their background, the chance to fulfill their potential.'